T. L. OSBORN

MIRACLES
PROOF of God's
Love

BOOKS BY THE OSBORNS

BELIEVERS IN ACTION — *Apostolic–Rejuvenating*

BIBLICAL HEALING — *Seven Miracle Keys*
4 Visions–60+ yrs. of Proof–324 Merged Bible Vs.

FIVE CHOICES FOR WOMEN WHO WIN
21st Century Options

GOD'S BIG PICTURE — *An Impelling Gospel Classic*

GOD'S LOVE PLAN — *The Awesome Discovery*

HEALING THE SICK — *A Living Classic*

JESUS & WOMEN — *Big Questions Answered*

LIFE–TRIUMPH OVER TRAGEDY (WHY)
A True Story of Life After Death

MIRACLES–PROOF OF GOD'S LOVE

NEW LIFE FOR WOMEN — *Reality Refocused*

NEW MIRACLE LIFE NOW — *For Asia and The World*
Global Communiqué of The Christian Faith

PEACE *IS A* LIFESTYLE — *Truths for Crisis Times*

SOULWINNING — *Outside The Sanctuary*
A Classic on Biblical Christianity & Human Dignity

THE BEST OF LIFE — *Seven Energizing Dynamics*

THE GOOD LIFE — *A Mini-Bible School–1,467 Ref.*

THE GOSPEL ACCORDING TO T.L. & DAISY
Their Life & World Ministry–510 pg. Pictorial

THE MESSAGE THAT WORKS
T.L.'s Revealing Manifesto on Biblical Faith

THE POWER OF POSITIVE DESIRE
An Invigorating Faith Perspective

THE WOMAN BELIEVER — *Awareness of God's Design*

WOMAN WITHOUT LIMITS
Unmuzzled — Unfettered — Unimpeded

WOMEN & SELF-ESTEEM — *Divine Royalty Unrestrained*

YOU ARE GOD'S BEST — *Transforming Life Discoveries*

OSBORN Ministries International

USA HQ:

OSBORN INTERNATIONAL

P.O. Box 10, Tulsa, OK 74102 USA

T.L. OSBORN, FOUNDER
LADONNA OSBORN, CEO

Tel: 918/743-6231
Fax: 918/749-0339   E-Mail: ministry@osborn.org
www.OSBORN.ORG

Canada: Box 281, Adelaide St. Post Sta., Toronto M5C 2J4
England: Box 148, Birmingham B3 2LG
(A Registered Charity)

BIBLE QUOTATIONS IN THIS BOOK MAY BE PERSONALIZED, PARAPHRASED, ABRIDGED OR CONFORMED TO THE *PERSON* AND *TENSE* OF THEIR CONTEXT IN ORDER TO FOSTER CLARITY AND INDIVIDUAL APPLICATION. VARIOUS LANGUAGE TRANSLATIONS AND VERSIONS HAVE BEEN CONSIDERED. BIBLICAL REFERENCES ENABLE THE READER TO COMPARE THE PASSAGES WITH HIS OR HER OWN BIBLE.

THE AUTHOR

ISBN 0-87943-140-2
Copyright 2003 by LaDonna C. Osborn
Printed in USA 2010-08
All Rights Reserved

Contents

MIRACLES

Proof of God's Love

"LOVE OF THE miraculous is not a mark of ignorance; rather it reveals humanity's intense desire to reach the unseen God."

T.L. Osborn

The Author

LaDonna, Osborn daughter

Preface

THE QUESTION IS often posed to me, "What makes your family so committed to helping people around the world?" The answer can be found on the pages of this book.

My mother and father (Drs. T.L. and Daisy Osborn) both accepted Christ at early ages and plunged into full time Christian ministry as newlyweds (ages 17 and 18). They were sincere in their faith, loyal in their associations, and zealous in their ministries. Yet when they faced the complexities of human need among the deeply religious people of India, it was evident that they had no valid response to the probing questions of people of other faiths. (The intriguing stories of T.L. and Daisy are available in their books THE GOSPEL ACCORDING TO T.L. AND DAISY, and BIBLICAL HEALING.)

When zealous actions failed, when human compassion was insufficient, when traditional doctrines were ineffective, and when all other options were exposed as powerless, my parents discovered the *MIRACLE* power of the resurrected Christ. Everything changed! Now after more than six decades of global ministry the issue of *MIRACLES* remains the pivotal reality of the Christian faith.

The year that I was born (1947) my parents began proclaiming and demonstrating the *MIRACLE* life of Jesus to people on every continent. We traveled as a family, living among unreached peoples of so many cultures and religions. (The final chapter of this book offers a brief overview of this ministry's impact on Christian missions in over 100 nations.)

My earliest memories as a child include being an eye witness to the awesome power of God's love toward people. Nothing is too hard for Him. No person is too beyond the reach of His compassion and rescue. No sickness is greater than His healing life. No wound or injustice is beyond His power to redeem and restore. *MIRACLES* are normal for God, who created all things by His great power and outstretched arm.

As a young adult I attended a Bible School. It was there that I heard for the first time that some Christians do not believe that *MIRACLES* are experienced today as they were in Bible days. I was shocked. To me the arguments and debates concerning *MIRACLES* were simply idle talk. I had seen thousands of *MIRACLES* of healing, of changed lives, of restored dreams, of reconciled relationships, of material provision, of physical protection, and more.

Today I continue the *MIRACLE* legacy of my parents through the various aspects of our global ministry. Nothing has changed, because the resurrected Jesus has not changed.

My eldest son, Tommy O'Dell, along with his wife Elisabeth and their children represent the next two generations of this family. Tommy's own story of conversion is a *MIRACLE* story. His supernatural encounter with Jesus is proof that when human effort reaches its limit, the *MIRACLE* power of Christ continues and accomplishes God's beautiful plan of rescue.

Tommy and Elisabeth have carried the gospel of Christ's *MIRACLE* life and power to over seventy nations of the world. Millions of souls have been saved in their crusades, and remarkable physical healings and other supernatural acts of our loving Lord have consistently confirmed their ministry.

It was Tommy who suggested that the book that you are holding, be reprinted and made available to this 21st Century generation. He wrote, "Within a few months of my conversion I happened upon the little book, *MIRACLES*, in my Grandmother's study. I began reading it aloud to myself. I think I had heard that when you accept printed material into your brain it affects you on one level but when you hear it spoken you receive it on another. So I decided to experiment with how deeply I could retain these simple truths. By the time I had finished the book, I was engulfed with the presence of God. I could no longer contain what felt like streams of electricity coursing through my body. When I was able to come to myself, I was astonished at this supernatural experience. I recognized that this book is special."

As you read these pages, you too will experience the *MIRACLE* of Christ's presence. He is alive. He loves you. He yearns to reveal Himself to you. Our entire family starting with my parents, continuing through me, extended to my sons and daughter, and now including my grandchildren, are committed to helping people know that God loves them and that His *MIRACLES* are *PROOF OF HIS LOVE* today! Only believe!

LaDonna Osborn,
D.Min., MA, BA, HLD, DD

MIRACLES—PROOF OF GOD'S LOVE

Tommy O'Dell

Introduction

By Tommy O'Dell
Son of Dr. LaDonna Osborn
Grandson of T.L. and Daisy Osborn
Founder: *FRONTIER EVANGELISM, Inc.*
8177 S. Harvard Ave. #222, Tulsa, OK 74137 USA

MIRACLES, *Proof of God's Power* (as this book was first titled) has been out of print for some years. I remember the spiritual experience that I had when I read my grandmother's copy many years ago.

I urged my grandfather to republish this book. He said, *"I will, if you will write an Introduction to it."* Then he asked me for some photos to include in this edition. My mother, Dr. LaDonna Osborn, has written the *Preface*.

Our family is committed to carrying

the gospel torch, and to sowing the seeds of truth in printed form, throughout our world. (My brother, Donald and his Argentine wife, Carina, have ministered in Romania, Indonesia, and are now raising up new churches in Ecuador.)

From the time that I first read this book and was baptized in the supernatural presence of Jesus, I have been privileged to carry this miracle gospel to over seventy nations of our hurting world.

While ministering in Holland, I met the lady who became my wife and partner in ministry. God has blessed us with five marvelous children. The older ones are already involved in our world ministry.

Elisabeth, my wife, and I instituted our world ministry — *FRONTIER EVANGELISM, Inc.* over twenty years ago. Through our mass evangelism crusades, millions of non-Christians have been born again, and the Lord has confirmed His word with thousands of miracles.

We are deeply grateful for the example that has been set by my grandparents, Drs. T.L. and Daisy, and by my mother, Dr. LaDonna Osborn. Her ministry is affecting nations around the globe.

I am thankful that this powerful little book is being republished. I hope you will not only read it, but will allow the Holy Spirit to brand these truths into your spirit until they produce in you indomitable *Hope*, unwavering *Faith*, and enduring *Love*.

Grandpa T.L. says: *"Christ died to redeem us so He can live in us. Now we express Him. He is our Spirit. We are His flesh. Together, that is a Christian."*

My Mother, Dr. LaDonna, wrote: *"Christ's passion drove Him to the cross. Now it drives believers to the lost. The world is the heart of the Church, and the Church is the hope of the world."*

That is what this little book, *MIRACLES*, is all about. It changed my life, and I believe it will change yours.

World Missionary Evangelist, Tommy O'Dell

Mary Kioko's son, George, at the tender age of seven was lifted from the scene of a terrifying accident and taken to the nearest hospital. Due to multiple fractures, he lay encased in a cast, from his ribs to his heels, for three torturous months. After agonizing years of bone fractures, casts, crutches and finally braces as well, he could only walk with the aid of crutches, steel braces and special shoes. In this condition, George was brought to the Osborn Crusade in Nakuru. It was a special miracle the young lad and his mother came expecting, and they were not disappointed. In just moments after Mr. Osborn prayed, **George was made whole**. What was correctly tagged by professionals as "impossible," became **possible** through simple child-like faith.

1

The Fact of Miracles

MINISTERS AND LAYMEN, both at home and abroad, often ask us to share with them the secrets which we consider most vital to reach the unevangelized millions of our generation. The answer to their question is found in the life and ministry of Christ and of the Early Church.

When Jesus began His public ministry, it was a ministry of miracles.

His conception, birth, life, wisdom and teachings, ministry, death, resurrection, appearances, and ascension—all were astounding and undeniable miracles.

When the Church began her ministry, it was a ministry of miracles.

A stream of miracles flowed from the hands of the Apostles, upsetting religious systems of that day to the extent that even the Christ-rejecting Roman government trembled.

The Church had made a discovery: Christ, whom God had raised from the dead, had the same power and worked the same miracles in response to their command, when given in His Name, as He did before He was condemned and killed. He was alive again! He lived in them! He had not changed!

In Jesus' Name, the sick were healed, the dead were raised, and demons were cast out!

Those first years of Early Church history, as recorded in the *Acts of the Apostles*, were example years for the *Acts of the Church* until the return of her Lord and Master. It was primitive Christianity, and it is unchanged today!

If we do not have the supernatural in Christianity, we have nothing to offer the unbeliever except a religion. True Christianity is not a religion.

Religion is a formality, a ritual, a ceremony. Biblical Christianity is *Life*.

Christianity is the heart and nature of Jesus Christ manifested and expressed in and through human persons.

Christianity is a miracle-life. It *began* in miracles; it is *based* on a succession of miracles; it is *propagated* by miracles. It is the only way of life that can satisfy the spiritual longing of men and women.

The Bible is a miracle book—a record of divine happenings. Beginning with Abraham, all of the major characters of Old Testament history were people who experienced miracles in response to their daring and active faith in God.

The purpose of these miracles was to separate the people from devotion to dead gods and to convert them to worship the Living God.

When miracles ended, the people lapsed into the veneration of other gods and only returned to the true and living God after another series of astounding miracles.

Human beings have not changed. I know because for over six decades, in over a hundred nations, our family has carried the gospel to millions, face-to-face. Multitudes of from 20,000 to 300,000 have thronged our meetings. Millions have turned to the Lord because of the miracles they have witnessed.

2

Everybody Wants a Miracle

Humanity yearns for the living God. Men and women crave a miracle.

Wherever there arises a man or woman whose prayers are heard and answered, greater crowds will flock to hear them than to hear the most famous philosopher or statesperson in the world.

This love of the miraculous is not a mark of ignorance. Rather, it reveals humanity's intense desire for rapport with the unseen God. Men and women want to see God in action.

The fact is that from the beginning, God's purpose and plan for humanity was that people have supernatural ability. They were created with the aspiration for supernatural authority. In Genesis 1:28, God said to the man and the woman whom He had created, *Subdue …and have dominion.*

Rationalists tell us that education will take the place of miracles, that the Church no longer needs the supernatural in Christianity. However education has never eliminated the yearning for the miraculous in the human species. Such arguments simply become the laughingstock of the Enemy.

One mighty miracle today, in the Name of Jesus Christ, is worth more than a lifetime of theoretical pedagogy.

Nations have never been rescued from their sins and reproaches by philosophical oratory or ecclesiastical indoctrination; but by humble men and women who have had a new vision of the living Christ, who is the *same yesterday, and to day, and for ever.*[Heb.13:8]

Every real spiritual awakening that has honored Christ and His Word has been attested by dynamic miracles. It is impossible to proclaim God's Word with biblical faith and not see miracles.

All normal people crave the supernatural. They long to see the manifestation of the power of God.

Even an atheistic professor who denies any existence of God will edge into the crowd to watch a miracle. A dead orthodoxy has no resurrection power within it, no miracle-working force back of it.

People are willing to put up with extravagances and some fanaticism in order to get a little touch of the supernatural God.

Cultured men and women will listen to an uneducated preacher because he or she has faith in the Living God—because he or she prays, and receives answers!

People tell us that we do not need miracles today, that education will take their place; but they are fooled by the Adversary, deluded by Satan. They reveal their lack of understanding of the nature and heart-hunger of men and women.

This yearning for the miraculous is deep-seated in humanity, regardless of nationality or background, because every human person is another offspring of the miracle God.

People want miracles today as much as they ever did. When they see God's Word confirmed by miracles, they know that it is true and they turn to the Lord in the same way that people did in Bible days. *Many believed in His name, when they saw the miracles which He did.*[Jn.2:23]

3

The Need for Miracles

JESUS CHRIST IS as much a miracle-worker now as He ever was; and humanity needs His miracle touch now more than ever.

Millions are yearning to rediscover the Christ-life. When He is allowed to live in people, in His power, in His love and in His personal presence, that is what biblical Christianity is all about. Religion without the miracle life of Christ is a ceremony, a ritual, a formality.

My Christian counsel is: *Embrace the Living, Miracle-working Christ.*

Wherever a man or a woman acts on God's Word in bold faith, the place will be crowded by throngs of people, eager to see Christ's miracle-performing power in evidence.

Jesus attracted the multitudes by miracles; and wherever miracles are wrought in His Name today, He does the same. *He is the same yesterday, today, and forever!*

When we return to Bible preaching, we can be assured of Bible results.

When we preach as the Early Church preached, we will get the same results, regardless of the area or the country in which we minister.

Unnumbered tens of thousands of Buddhists, Shintoists, Hindus, Muslims, fetish worshippers, and followers of other religions have believed on Jesus Christ and turned to Him in our crusades around the world, because they saw the proof of His living presence, and the reality of His Word in action through the miracles which He wrought.

4

Foundation for Miracles

THE BIBLE SAYS, *Faith comes by hearing...the word of God.*Rom.10:17

Today, faith may *leave* by hearing the word of unbelieving theologians, and unbelief may *come* by listening to philosophical traditionalists.

A week of fasting may be proclaimed, but this will not bring the miraculous into evidence if the biblical promises of God are not taught and believed.

Nights of prayer may be arranged, but it will be of no avail if the preaching or teaching is not focused on Jesus who is *the same yesterday, today and forever.*Heb.13:8

Spiritual awakening must begin in the speaker, the teacher, the leader. The message must be right, or all else is empty.

The messenger, at home or abroad, must be willing to conform his or her thinking, preaching and actions to biblical principles of redemptive truth. Otherwise, spiritual renewal under his or her leadership will never be experienced.

Faith comes by hearing…the word of God, Rom.10:17 – not by teaching philosophical and outdated religious traditions.

Jesus told the Pharisees that they were *making the word of God of none effect through their traditions.*Mk.7:13

Unless the preacher, the missionary, or the leader is willing to surrender ideas, or methods, or teaching, or traditions which are not biblical, then spiritual awakening cannot develop under his or her leadership. If someone does not receive new spiritual understanding from God, their enthusiasm will likely be suppressed.

We cannot teach obsolete, traditional religious concepts and experience Bible results. We cannot practice outdated missionary policies and expect to convince non-Christians about Christ.

If we want to reap the fruit of faith, we must sow the *seed* of faith, which is *the Word of God.*[Lu.8:11]

The sick will be healed, non-Christians will be converted, and unbelievers will turn to Christ in any locality, when the gospel in its simplicity is communicated. When actions correspond with that teaching, it opens the way for Christ in His power to confirm His Word.

When we proclaim biblical truth, we open the way for the miraculous.

Jesus said, *You shall know the truth, and the truth shall make you free.*[Jn.8:32]

God sent His Word and it healed them.[Psa. 107:20] Young's translation says, *He sends His word and heals them* — present tense. He is doing that *now.*

God's promises are *life to those that find them, and health to all their flesh.*[Prov.4:22]

God's Word is His voice speaking to you individually. Read His promises in the Bible. Accept and embrace them personally — as though the Lord were having a private conversation with you.

Do whatever He tells you to do and expect Him to do what He says He will do. That is the meaning of real living faith.

Believe His promises. Think about them. Ponder them in your mind. Speak them with your lips. Act upon them in simple child-like faith and God will fulfill them in your life by a miracle today — now.

5

Ministry of Miracles

AMONGST THE THOUSANDS at home and abroad who have been miraculously healed by our Lord in our meetings, only a small percentage of them have been individually prayed for. Most have been healed through their own faith which was created in their own hearts while meditating on the Bible truths we shared from the platform or from the printed page.

In over a hundred nations during six decades of world ministry, we have discovered that almost any member of any church knows about Paul's thorn, Job's boils, Timothy's sore stomach, the teaching of sickness as God's chastisement, and the idea of suffering sickness for the glory of God.

But very few of them can quote a Bible verse that promises healing. This is because preachers, missionaries, and teachers have not informed the people about these vital promises.

Obviously they have not taught God's covenant of healing, His promises that reveal the believer's position of authority over Satan and Satan-made diseases, the Christian's biblical assurance that if they *ask*, they will *receive*,[Mat.7:7] Satan's legal defeat by Christ in His death for us on the cross, the believer's true ministry, how Christ bore our diseases and pains, or our legal rights to health and abundant living.

Instead, they have taught reasons for not being healed, and concepts that God uses sickness for His glory and for the loving chastisement of His children.

Without knowledge of the positive truths of healing that abound in the scriptures, one has nothing upon which to base his or her faith for physical healing.

If preachers or missionaries or teachers do not teach these truths, the people cannot know them.

If the people do not know them, there can be no faith for miracles.

If there is no faith, miracles will not be wrought.

If miracles are not wrought, there is nothing to draw unbelievers and non-Christians to hear the gospel, nor to persuade them to believe it.

We must recognize the indisputable value of miracles! They are a *witness* of God's power—*evidence* of the truth of the gospel.

Without miracles, Christianity is no more than another religion or a philosophy. Real Christianity is neither. *It is a LIFE!*

Biblical Christianity is the *only* form of worship in which the object worshipped dwells in the heart of the worshipper.

No Hindu, Shintoist, Muslim or Buddhist ever claimed that the deity worshipped dwells in the worshipper. Such a concept would be considered sacrilegious in most non-Christian religions.

Yet, that is precisely the essence of *Christianity* – Jesus dwelling in the heart of the believer, by faith. *Christ IN YOU, the hope of glory.*[Col.1:27]

Miracles wrought in the Name of Jesus Christ are evidence that Christ is risen from the dead according to the Scriptures. If He is risen, He will do the same things that He did before He was crucified. ***Miracles are the proof.***

6

Miracles As Evidence

*A*ND THIS GOSPEL *of the Kingdom shall be preached in all the world for a witness unto all nations and then shall the end come.*^{Mat.24:14}

These words were spoken by Jesus Christ to His disciples in answer to their questions: *Tell us, what shall be the sign of your coming, and of the end of the world?* ^{v.3}

He told them to beware of deceivers and of those who claim to be Christ. He said that they would hear of wars, earthquakes, and pestilence; that some of them would be hated and even killed for His Name's sake; that there would be false prophets and that the love of many would wax cold because of abounding iniquity.

Then, after all of those signs, He gave them the main sign of His coming: *This gospel of the Kingdom shall be preached in all the world for a witness unto all nations; and then shall the end come.*

When over half of the inhabitants of the world have not yet heard Christ's message, and have not received a single page of *the gospel in their language,* we cannot say that this sign has been fulfilled.

Jesus said, *The gospel must first be published among all nations.*Mk.13:10

The accomplishment of this task is the priority of every Christian believer.

The ripened harvest of millions of souls will be swept into darkness unless Christians respond quickly. Our mission is to share the Good News with our hurting world—to give them an opportunity to know about Christ and His love for them. *The gospel must first be published among all nations.*Mk.13:10

Why should *anyone* hear the gospel repeatedly before *everyone* has heard it once?

The *supreme* task of the Church is the *evangelization of the world*.

That was Christ's final commission to His followers—the purpose for which He sent the power of His Holy Spirit into their lives.[Ac.1:8]

I have already dedicated over six decades of my life to proclaim this gospel to people around the world, and I shall continue doing so as long as I live and am capable of action.

For years, we published more than a ton of gospel literature every day, in 132 languages, and shipped them to Christian workers around the world.

We have sponsored over 30,000 national preachers as full-time missionaries to unevangelized tribes and villages. For many years, more than 400 new self-supporting churches have been established *annually*.

We have provided millions of books, tens of thousands of crusade sermon tapes, CDs, videos and DocuMiracle films around the world — in 70 major languages, plus continuing our own mass miracle campaigns. Why? Our mission is to reach the world with *this gospel of the Kingdom* that Jesus and the Apostle Paul talked so much about.

7

Gospel of Miracles

WHAT IS *THIS GOSPEL of the Kingdom?*

It is the same gospel that Jesus Christ preached, the same that His disciples and the apostles proclaimed.

When Jesus authorized His disciples to go forth, He said, *As ye go, preach, saying, the Kingdom of heaven is at hand.*Mat.10:7

With that message, He told them: H*eal the sick, cleanse the lepers, raise the dead, cast out devils: freely ye have received, freely give.*Mat.10:7-8 These miracles were evidence of *this gospel of the Kingdom.*Mat.24:14

Jesus went about all the cities and villages teaching in their synagogues, and preaching the gospel of the kingdom, and healing every

sickness and every disease among the people.
Mat.9:35

When He preached *the gospel of the King-dom*, He *always* healed the sick.

And he was casting out a devil...and it came to pass, when the devil was gone out ...the people wondered.[Lu.11:14] And Jesus said, *If I cast out devils by the Spirit of God, then the Kingdom of God is come unto you.*
Mat.12:28

Jesus proved that when *the gospel of the Kingdom* is preached, devils are cast out and the sick are healed.

It is *this gospel of the Kingdom* — preached in the power of the Holy Spirit, confirmed by signs and wonders and divers miracles, that is persuading millions of non-Christians to believe on Jesus Christ as their savior and Lord.

In recent years, nation after nation is witnessing the miraculous manifestation of Jesus Christ in action.

We pioneered *Mass Miracle Evangelism.* We were the first to go out on a field, in a non-Christian nation and erect a big platform, then to invite the public to come and to see for themselves if the Bible is true, if Jesus Christ is alive, and if His promises are good today.

That is what we do in every crusade that we conduct. We never lay hands on the people or try to touch them. (That can precipitate a riot in a mass of people.)

We announce *this gospel of the Kingdom* and publicly teach Christ's promises to save and to heal. We proclaim that Jesus came to show us God's love; that He assumed our sins and endured our judgment by dying in our place on the cross so that we can have His *Gift of Life*; that He bore our sicknesses and diseases so that we can be healed and experience His health in our bodies.

Then we invite all who believe the gospel to receive Jesus as savior. We lead the multitudes in a mass confession of faith in Christ, then in thanksgiving for His gift of salvation.

Then we pray for God to express His

divine love to the people by healing them if they are sick. God always answers that prayer. Those who receive miracles come to the platform and give public witness. *Every miracle is more proof of God's love* and is more evidence that the Bible is true.

Today, men and women are emulating our example, preaching to multitudes—not in just one country, but in nations around the world.

God is confirming the Word preached with signs and wonders, and a return to apostolic faith in God is the result.

In a recent crusade, a leper was cleansed by a miracle of God. Her hands and feet had degenerated so that nothing was left but stubs. Also, the disease has affected her spine so that to move about, she had to crawl on her knees and stubbed hands. She begged at the big market gateway.

She was instantly cured the first night she attended our crusade. The next day, thousands jammed the streets and the city was in an exultant uproar as Miriam Gare walked and ran (on her stubbed legs), glorifying God publicly. Her flesh was clean and pure again.

We assisted in having her fitted with special shoes and the District Commissioner wrote to tell us that this notable miracle had caused the entire district to know that Christ is alive today.

That is *this gospel of the Kingdom.*

8

Missions and Miracles

IN 1945, MY WIFE AND I, with our baby boy, sailed to India as missionaries, with a burning desire to preach and teach the gospel of Christ to people of a non-Christian nation.

Though we had no previous experience abroad, the Holy Spirit was guiding us. Since we could not speak the language, our plan was to engage a national interpreter so that we could begin ministering at once.

We planned to erect a big palm-leaf arbor where the people could assemble, providing a cover from the sun for extra meetings during the day. We would teach the gospel and win the Hindus to Christ. With the new converts, we would establish new churches. If we had done that, success would have been inevitable.

But the senior missionaries obliged us to conform our activities to traditional concepts. Our fresh ideas were labeled *Americanisms,* inappropriate for India. Our priority must be to learn the language. That would take at least two years, and we were told not to expect to engage in ministry during our first term in India.

This prospect was disheartening to us, but having had no previous experience abroad, we tried to convince ourselves that they knew best.

Throughout the winter, we did nothing but study an occasional lesson in Hindustani. Once each week I was sent to the little mission hall that seated about 20 persons, to print on a small blackboard the title of the sermon to be delivered by the senior missionary.

There was no vision. The mission was opened only once a week—on Sundays at 6:00 pm for an hour-and-a-half. The meeting was normally attended by about a dozen persons.

In our desperation to escape this hopeless outlook, we sold some of our meager belongings for enough money to go to another city where another missionary, knowing of our success in evangelism in the USA, invited us for two weeks of special meetings. We imagined beautiful success.

But when we arrived, we encountered a similar situation. The doors of the little store-front mission, that they called their church, were opened at six o'clock on Sunday evening when, for a short time, a small group of Christians gathered to go through their usual routine. That was "missionary" thinking at that time.

Before our "series of meetings" began, the missionary instructed me that I should not invite people to come forward to accept Christ. He explained: "We do things differently here than in America."

For two weeks, after my gospel message, the missionary stepped to the pulpit, raised his hand and solemnly pronounced a formal benediction, dismissing the people. No results were expected, and none could take place.

On the closing night, I decided that despite the senior missionary's objection, I would give the listeners an opportunity to receive Christ.

At the close of my message, I shocked the missionary by calling for those who wanted to receive Christ as savior, to come forward, to kneel, and that I would lead them in prayer to receive the Lord Jesus as their Lord and Savior. Eleven Indians responded in tears and accepted Christ.

The missionary was so upset that he walked out of the meeting. Upon reaching his residence after the service, we found his wife cautiously making the point: "Honey, the meeting tonight proves that if we preach and do the same as we do in America, the same results will take place here in India."

As I recall the painful experiences of trying to adjust to the hopeless and non-productive "missionary" thinking that prevailed in that epoch, I have one regret. Although we were so very young and had no previous experience outside the USA, I regret that I allowed others to divert us from the ideas that God had impressed upon us for ministry in India. We would have had great success, would have established many new churches, and would have won many souls to Christ, because India is no different.

After only ten months, we returned to the United States because we realized that, under those circumstances, we could never convince non-Christians that Jesus Christ is alive. We realized that we needed miracles to prove His power and we had not learned the biblical truths that produce the healing wonders of Christ in action.

After returning home, we fasted and prayed for many days searching for the answer to our agonizing spiritual dilemma. We had seen the masses and their empty search for "The Omnipotent One."

We knew that, if non-Christians were to be convinced about Christ, a new breed of gospel messengers must be birthed, who would preach and demonstrate His miracle working power and love for this generation.

We believed in miracles but we did not know the truths that would bring about their manifestation in our ministry. It was clear to us that if the blind could be made to see, the deaf to hear, the lame to walk, and if lepers could be cleansed, multiplied thousands would believe on the Lord and would be saved.

At that epoch, Christian leaders seemed to relegate miracles to Bible times, while the masses of humanity lived and died without ever hearing a gospel message confirmed by signs, miracles and wonders.

We felt alone, helpless, and defeated. But, thank God, we did not abandon hope. We knew that the real *mission* of Jesus Christ in the world was a *mission* of *miracles*. So we prayed and fasted and God heard our prayers.

9

Jesus of Miracles

ONE MORNING, Jesus appeared to me. It was an awesome experience. I knew He was alive and that He was the same as He was in Bible days. From that moment, Jesus became *Lord* in my life.

Shortly after that experience, a man with a powerful miracle ministry came to Portland, Oregon, where we had become the pastors of a church.

As we witnessed the miracles wrought by Christ during that man's biblical ministry, we knew that God would do the same miracles through any man or woman who would proclaim His promises and who would dare to act upon His written Word recorded in the sacred scriptures.

We determined to re-read the Gospels — as though we had never read them before. We resolved to act on His word, to do what He told us to do, and to expect Him to do what He said He would do.

As God began to manifest His miracles in our ministry across America, the unevangelized masses of other nations again seemed to cry to us for hope in God. With Christ's miraculous power in evidence — healing the sick and casting out devils — we knew the people in non-Christians nations would believe on Christ by the thousands.

We had observed in India that the philosophical religions of the masses offered them no hope, and no healing.

Since we arrived at those conclusions, our family has proclaimed the gospel of Jesus Christ in over a hundred nations. Non-productive, obsolete "missionary" methods of colonial epochs have never again been permitted to impede our miracle gospel ministry.

Instead, we have done, in nation after nation, what God impressed us to do in India. We have engaged interpreters to translate our preaching, line by line, into the language of the people. We have proclaimed Christ and His miracle gospel to many millions of non-Christians, influencing them to believe the gospel of Jesus Christ, and to embrace Him as their Lord and savior.

The results have been overwhelming: Many hundreds of thousands of souls have accepted Christ. As in Bible days, *great multitudes followed Him, because they saw His miracles which He did on them that were diseased.*[Jn.6:2]

Jesus said, *This gospel of the Kingdom shall be preached in all the world, as a witness to all nations, then shall the end come.* Mat.24:14

Our ministry was gloriously rejuvenated from the day that we learned that Jesus Christ wanted to *confirm* His gospel that we would preach, just as He confirmed His followers (after His resurrection).[Mk.16:20]

In these many nations, every crusade we have conducted has been triumphant —from Estonia to El Salvador, from Nigeria to New Guinea, from Asia to Austria, from India to Indonesia, from Poland to Panama, from Eurasia to Uganda, from Brazil to Bulgaria, from Africa to Australia, from Kenya to Kyrgyzstan, from Europe to the USA. The people of every nation have responded exactly the same.

We have constructed our platforms out on large fields or parks or in stadiums—out where people of all religions can assemble freely. We have kept our message simple: *Jesus Christ is the same yesterday, and to day, and for ever.*[Heb.13:8]

We have told the multitudes what happened to those who came to Jesus Christ in Bible days. Our message has been: *Come to Him like they came, believe on Him like they believed, call on Him like they called, cry like they cried, repent like they repented, pray like they prayed, act like they acted,* **and you will receive what they received.**

Many tens of thousands of needy and lonely people have been saved and healed as a result, because **the *Jesus of Miracles* has never changed.**

The redemptive blessing of *Biblical Healing* is available to all who believe that Christ assumed the judgment of our sins and of their consequences in order to restore us to God as though we had never sinned. No crime can be punished twice. No debt can be paid twice. He acted on our behalf. We are free. He arose from the dead and returned to restore God's Life to us. *Christ Himself bare our sins in His own body on the tree* [1 Pe. 2:24] [and He] *took our infirmities and bare our sicknesses*, [Mt 8:17] [so that] *by His stripes we are healed.* [1 Pe. 2:24; Isa. 52:5]

OSBORN CRUSADES

AFRICA

S. AMERICA

INDONESIA

CARIBBEAN

PHILIPPINES

THE
HAROLD KHAN
MIRACLE

Harold's right leg was five inches shorter than his left one. The photo below shows both legs perfectly equal after his miraculous healing which took place as he listened to T.L.'s gospel message and believed on Christ. (His right elevated shoe and left leg brace are now obsolete.)

Both Harold's mother (standing with him above) and his father (devout Muslims) accepted Christ as their Savior and Lord.

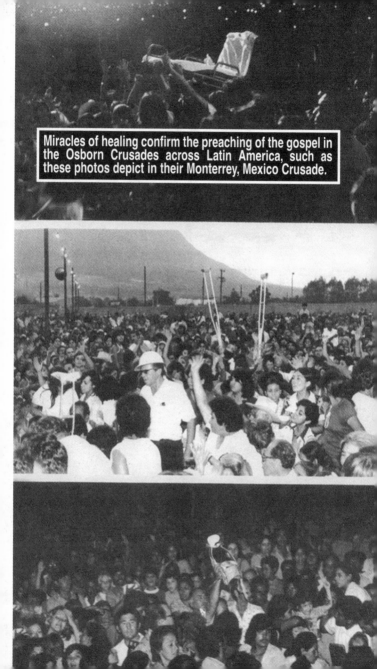

Miracles of healing confirm the preaching of the gospel in the Osborn Crusades across Latin America, such as these photos depict in their Monterrey, Mexico Crusade.

Her leg was 4 inches shorter than the other, and paralyzed – the result of a birth defect. She was instantly healed in the Osborn Crusade at Bogota, Colombia.

Crippled by polio when he was a lad, this Hindu man could never move about except by scooting on his hips. He was known as the "Frog Man" beggar. During the Osborns' histori Lucknow, India crusade, the man was instantly healed.

OSBORN CRUSADE

Crippled by Infantile Paralysis, Shanti Sundram could only walk with a hip-to-ankle brace. One leg was 3 inches shorter than the other. She was miraculously healed during the Osborn Crusade at Madurai, India. (Top) Her mother thanks God for this miracle.

MADURAI, INDIA

"We're bringing hope and faith to tens of thousands who have known nothing but Godless communism."
– T.L. and daughter LaDonna Osborn

Osborns bring miracle life to thousands of Ukrainians.

Kharkov, Ukraine auditorium is packed for Osborns' Ministry.

LaDonna shocks Kharkov with her dynamic preaching. Seeing her preach with power, then pray with faith, and seeing miracles manifested, is evidence to these tough people that God does not limit women in ministry.

T.L. & LaDonna Osborn Miracle Crusade – Medellin, Colombia.

LaDonna Osborn

T.L. & LaDonna Osborn Miracle-Life Conference–Amlaty, Kyrghyzstan, an ex-Soviet Republic. The 10 Osborn books in Russian are given to every adult.

Osborn Mass Miracle Crusade – Bogota, S. America

Thousands attend the T.L. & LaDonna Osborn Miracle Life Conference in this ancient Muslim nation of Kyrghyzstan – bordering West China.

T.L. Osborn

Osborn proclaims the living gospel in 4 cities of Poland. 15 TONS of Osborn books in Polish are given to the people.

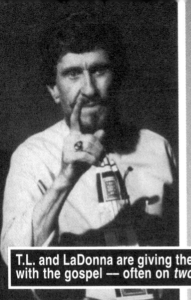

T.L. and LaDonna are giving their BEST to reach nations with the gospel — often on *two fronts at once.*

T.L. Osborn proclaims the gospel to thousands in Lithuania where communism dominated since Lenin's Godless revolution. Today the new church is on the rise.

As Bishop of over 700 pastors and churches, LaDonna believes that each soul won to Christ must be attracted into a local church where they can grow in the grace and knowledge of Christ to become His love-carriers to others.

As an Evangelist, LaDonna's life is involved in sharing Christ with the world. She ministers to multitudes with the same anointing that has rested upon her parents, T.L. & Daisy. She lives with a passion to reach the UNreached.

T.L. and LaDonna, believe the priority of every church and of each believer is to share Christ's love with *"every creature."*

With the heart of a crusader, the commitment of a pastor, the experience of an ambassador, and the anointing of an apostle, Bishop LaDonna is a proclaimer of Redemptive truth to the peoples of her world.

Preacher

Teacher

Leader

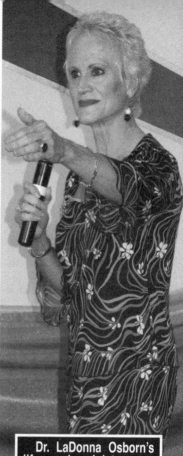

Dr. LaDonna Osborn's life and ministry are focused on reaching the UNreached, then on building each convert into the Body of Christ.

As Bishop of more than 700 pastors and churches, her passion is to see that each soul won to Christ becomes part of a local church where they learn to function as His representative in sharing His love with others.

Dr. LaDonna, in Beijing, dedicates tons of T.L.'s book, *"Healing the Sick"*, in Mandarin Chinese language.

One fifth of the world lives in China. *"Why should anyone hear the gospel twice before everyone has heard it once?"* We are seeding China NOW.

Osborn books in Mandarin, seeding for China's great soul harvest.

China has influenced the world for over 5,000 years. Now, the *old* is giving way to the *new*. God's LOVE and redemptive plan for humanity is the only hope for these millions.

In between campaigns, Tommy O'Dell shares stories of the continuing epic of 'The Book of Acts' with his grandfather, Dr. T.L. Osborn.

Tommy O'Dell's 'Frontier Evangelism' ministry organization ministers the gospel to this receptive African crowd.

Jesus opens the eyes of the blind in this Tommy O'Dell Crusade in Natitingou, Benin.

"Last night when I was coming from my home I could barely walk. On the advertisement it said that Evangelist O'Dell was going to pray for the sick. I went to the crusade and after the Evangelist prayed I was free! And this morning I was more free than yesterday!"

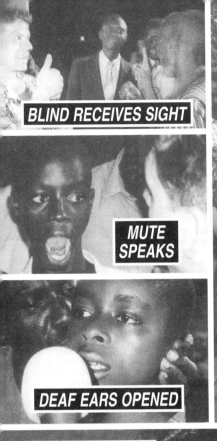

BLIND RECEIVES SIGHT

MUTE SPEAKS

DEAF EARS OPENED

TUMOR VANISHES

CRIPPLE HEALED, RUNS AS PROOF

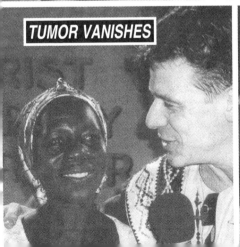

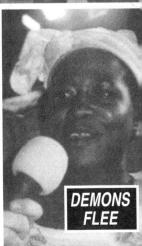

DEMONS FLEE

Evangelist Tommy O'Dell preaches (left) and prays (right) for the people who attend his meetings. (Below) A few of the mass crusades that have assembled in his ministry to over 70 nations.

Tommy O'Dell preaching the gospel with interpreter Tanya Logvinovich.

Left to right: Jesse & Deedee, Tommy Ray & Elisabeth, Donovan, Jerry, Madalena, Andresa & Tommy Lee. Inset: Tommy's first grandchild, Genesis Anabella.

Tommy is an accomplished musician, and uses every opportunity to convey the Good News message through music.

Tommy poses in front of a rickshaw on one of his many evangelism trips. He has victoriously ministered Christ's saving and healing power in over 70 countries for over two decades.

This blind Muslim man attended Tommy O'Dell's crusade. During the crusade he accepts Christ and gains his sight. He expresses his thanks to Rev. O'Dell for God's miracle provision.

"For six decades we have been the bridge between *Christians who care*, but have no *channel*—and the *unreached who hope*, but have no *messenger*."

We are thankful for believing Christians and leaders who choose us as their *Partners* in reaching the UNreached with the gospel.
Dr. T.L. Osborn and daughter, *Dr. LaDonna Osborn*

10

Miracles As Proof

JESUS SAID, *This gospel of the Kingdom shall be preached in all the world for a WITNESS to all nations; and then shall the end come.*^{Mat.24:14} I noticed one day that the word *witness* in the original Bible text means *"something evidential; with proof or with evidence."* In a court case, the *witness who brings evidence* is the winner.

This discovery increased the assurance in my heart that our ministry today should emulate the ministry of Jesus Christ.

He went about all the cities and villages, teaching…and preaching the gospel of the Kingdom, and healing every sickness and every disease among the people.^{Mat.9:35}

*His fame spread abroad, and great multi-tudes came together to hear and to be healed by Him of their infirmities...and as He was teaching...the power of the Lord was present to heal.*Lu.5:15,17

We became thoroughly convinced that *this gospel of the Kingdom, with evidence* would convince the peoples of non-Christian religions (and of no religion) that the Bible is true, that Jesus Christ is alive and unchanged today.

John the Baptist sent disciples to observe the ministry of Jesus, and to inquire as to whether or not He was the Christ. The Lord sent them back with this answer: *Go and shew John the things that you hear and see: the blind receive their sight, and the lame walk, the lepers are cleansed, and the deaf hear, the dead are raised up, and the poor have the gospel preached to them.*Mat.11:4-5

They *heard* the gospel preached.

They *saw* the blind receive their sight.

They *saw* the lame walk.

They *saw* the miracles!

Jesus' message was not only *spoken*, but it was announced *with evidence*. His gospel was with *proof!* His preaching was with *demonstration!*

He was the Christ, and the miracles proved it.

Christian messengers have gone throughout the world, but not enough of them have *demonstrated* what they have preached. Consequently, many of them have experienced meager results.

On the other hand, where men and women have proclaimed Christ in all of His love and power, non-Christians have responded and have believed on Christ, embracing Him as Lord.

Jesus stated: *This gospel of the Kingdom shall be preached in all the world FOR A WITNESS to all nations.*Mat.24:14 It is always the witness who brings *proof* that convinces the court and wins the case.

When Philip went to the city of Samaria, he *preached Christ unto them. And the people with one accord gave heed to what Philip said,* **hearing and seeing the** *miracles which he did. For unclean spirits ...came out of many that were possessed with them: and many taken with palsies, and that were lame, were healed.*Ac.8:5-8

Philip preached Christ *with evidence.* His message was confirmed by miracles, and the miracles were the *witn*ess that convinced the people of the city.

Miracles *testified* that what Philip taught was *the truth.*

It was not enough to *hear* the message, nor is that enough today. The people of Samaria needed to *see* the miracles which bore *evidence* that Philip was speaking the truth. Today, it is the miracles that *witness* to the truth of the gospel.

11

Urgency of Miracles

REMEMBER: *Evidence* is essential to winning the case.

More can be accomplished through a single message of biblical gospel confirmed by miracles than by years of teaching without supernatural proof.

Paul testified that *Christ wrought mighty signs and wonders through him by the power of the Spirit of God, which made the Gentiles obedient by* **word** *and* **deed**.^{Rom. 15:18-19}

The Bible says that *our great salvation which was first spoken by the Lord, and was* **confirmed** *unto us by them that heard him* — God also **bearing them witness, both with signs and wonders, and with divers miracles,** *and gifts of the Holy Ghost.* Heb.2:3-4

The gospel was *with evidence.* The message was *with proof.*

The unbelieving world needs to hear Christian messengers who, like Paul, preach *not with enticing words of human wisdom, but **in demonstration of the Spirit and of power:** so that the people's faith will not stand in human wisdom, but in **the power of God**.*[1Cor.2:4,5]

For unbelievers to be convinced about Christ and His gospel, they must *hear* His teaching and *see* it confirmed by miracles that give **witness of the truth spoken.**

People of any nation will follow messengers of daring faith whose preaching is coupled with the confirmation of signs and miracles as *evidence* – as a *witness*, of the Living Christ.

A Catholic priest attended one of our crusades. It was his first time to see the message of the gospel confirmed by miracles. He was captivated by the simplicity of it all. Out among the people, standing on the field, in deep repentance for his sins and unbelief, he fell on his face, and was gloriously *born again*.

He gave his witness before the multitude of 75,000 people. In a weeping and trembling voice, he said: *When I came to this field, I saw no golden altar, no candlesticks and no professional ecclesiastic. All I saw was a vast field of people, a crude, wooden platform, a Bible, and a preacher of childlike faith in God. I saw Jesus Christ through that messenger – I saw Him confirming His gospel with biblical miracles. Now I know that the Christ of the Bible is more than a religion. He is alive and real.*

A missionary of a historical church organization attended our crusade in his city. At the end, he witnessed to the multitude: *More souls have been saved in these three weeks than in thirty years of our missionary activities without miracles.*

12

The Miracle Witness

I SHALL NEVER FORGET how my life was changed when I discovered that the Bible word *witness* is the word used to describe the Old Testament *"Tabernacle of Witness."* There Jehovah-God met with the people of Israel ^{Ex.25:8;29:45-46} during their wilderness journey to the *Promised Land*.

That tent was called the *"Tabernacle of Witness"* because for twenty-four hours of every day, God's miraculous power and presence was in evidence there.

Other nations could build tents. They could collect and use the same materials, but the glory of God's presence — His miraculous *witness* would not be there.

Continually, God was present. His

glory was in evidence. It was the *"Tabernacle of **Witness**."* Ex.29:43

Jesus said, *You shall receive power, after the Holy Ghost is come upon you: and ye shall be **witnesses** unto me.* Ac.1:8

Paul wrote, *Know ye not that your body is the temple of the Holy Ghost?* 1Cor.6:19

Now WE ARE *HIS WITNESSES.* We are *Tabernacles of Witness.* God wills that His miraculous power be perpetually manifested in evidence in our lives. We bear Holy Ghost *testimony.*

The Apostles Peter and John received the power and anointing of the Holy Ghost. They lifted a crippled man to his feet *in the name of Jesus Christ of Nazareth.* Ac.3:1-6 Their faith and action gave *witness* – *proof* of the resurrection of Christ.

As a result of their *witness in action*, they were arrested, and required to explain the power or the name by which they performed this wonder. Peter stood before the court of official religious dignitaries and declared: *"We are His witnesses!"* Ac.5:32

Others may preach; they may deliver

their lectures; but if they lack God's supernatural *power to witness* for Christ—if their words are not confirmed by His miracle power, then their message is not convincing.

It is God's will that His miraculous presence be manifested in and through our lives in order for our words to be confirmed.

It is one thing to say, "I am a theologian." It is another thing to say, "I am *Christ's witness.*"

The greatest honor and calling on earth, is to be a *witness* for Jesus Christ—to be endued with His Holy Spirit in order to *preach the gospel in demonstration of the Spirit and of power.*[1Cor.2:4]

Biblical, apostolic Christianity has always been promulgated by *witnesses, confessors, testifiers*—by messengers who have met Jesus Christ and have experienced His love and power in their lives.

The early Christians were *commanded* [by official opposers] *not to speak at all nor teach in the name of Jesus.*[Ac.4:18]

But they *answered… Whether it be right in the sight of God to hearken to you more than to God, you judge. But we can only speak* [or witness of] *the things that we have* **seen** *and* **heard**.[Ac.4:19,20]

That is the *miracle witness* we are to give to our world. That is why the power of the Holy Ghost has been imparted to believers. They become *"Tabernacles of Witness"* through whom God's power and glory is manifested, giving proof that Jesus Christ is alive, real, and present — in the now.

13

Miracles for Multitudes

THE GOSPEL SAYS, *Christ's followers went forth, and preached every where, the Lord working with them, and confirming the word with signs following.*Mk 16:20

They were messengers *with evidence.* What they taught was *demonstrated!* The gospel preached by them was their *witness.* They were preachers with power — full of God, full of faith, full of the Holy Ghost. They were *witnesses* for Christ.

Modern theologians often argue that one can believe on the Lord and be saved, but they often teach against the supernatural and some even deny that miracles can be experienced today.

Unbelieving religious leaders, during the epoch of the Early Church, were frustrated and even infuriated by learning that Paul or Peter had come to their area.

When they arrived in town, the public outcry was: *These that have turned the world upside down have come here also.*[Ac. 17:6] And their words were not a compliment.

When we arrived in a certain nation, Protestant missionaries from the United States, oblivious to God's miracle ministry abroad, began a campaign to influence national pastors against us. They contended: "This man Osborn will bring division and confusion. It would be better if he had never come to our area."

They went from pastor to pastor, in their concerted effort to prevent our great public campaign from taking place. Some pastors were influenced by their accusations, but most of the national churches enthusiastically participated with us, and their churches overflowed with hundreds of new converts.

Many miracles, signs, and wonders were wrought which gave proof of the gospel that we preached. Thousands of people accepted Christ as their savior.

Wherever messengers of the Early Church declared the gospel, Christ confirmed their message with miraculous signs and wonders.

Whether it was Peter in Jerusalem,[Ac.5:14-16] Philip in Samaria,[Ac.8:5-8] or Paul on the pagan island of Melita,[Ac.28:1-9] the same results were experienced: They proclaimed the gospel, miracles gave proof of what they taught, and multitudes believed and were added to the Church.

Their sermons were *demonstrated.*

Their preaching was *with power.*

They were *Christ's witnesses.*[Ac.1:8]

14

Questions about Miracles

WHAT KIND OF BIBLE would we have without Moses leading the people of God out of Egyptian slavery, through the Red Sea, and into the Promised Land? Or without Elijah raising the dead and calling down fire from heaven?

What kind of Bible would we have without Daniel praying in the lions' den and being unharmed, or without the three Hebrew children having faith to be delivered from a fiery furnace?

What kind of gospel would we have without Christ healing the sick, cleansing the lepers, raising the dead, and giving sight to the blind?

What kind of Early Church would we

have without Peter raising the cripple to his feet so he could walk again, then gathering the sick on beds and on couches in the main streets of Jerusalem when *they were healed everyone*? Ac.5:15-16

What kind of example would Paul be without healing the sick, commanding the impotent man to arise, and casting the devils out of the fortune-telling woman?

What kind of "Great Commission" would we have without Christ's command to cast out devils in His Name and to lay hands on the sick for their recovery?

Remove these promises and these miracles from the Bible and what is left? Nothing more than another philosophical religion.

What kind of preacher or theologian is it that opposes the supernatural in gospel ministry?

What kind of preaching and teaching is it that discredits the miraculous as being irrelevant to the gospel message?

What kind of missionary ministers

abroad, but opposes the miraculous in Christianity today?

Without the manifestation of God's power, what remains is a ritual of religious worship, a collection of dogmas and creeds, a philosophy of concepts that give no life, solve no problems, heal no sicknesses, and produce no new births in the Kingdom of God.

Jesus spoke in tough terms when He said: *Woe unto you, scribes and Pharisees, hypocrites! For you compass sea and land to make one proselyte, and when he is made, you make him twofold more the child of hell than yourselves.*[Mat.23:15]

Let us embrace an unyielding resolve that the gospel with *evidence* shall be our message. We shall go forth and proclaim the gospel—*this gospel of the Kingdom.* We shall be *witnesses with proof* and we shall reap a harvest of lost souls for Christ as our reward.

That is what we have done for over six decades in over a hundred nations.

From one extremity of this globe to the

other, the signs and miracles which have confirmed the gospel that we proclaim have caused multitudes of non-Christians to believe on Jesus Christ and to embrace Him as Savior and Lord of their lives.

That is our mission: *to open their eyes, and to turn them from darkness to light, and from the power of Satan unto God, that they may receive forgiveness of sins.*[Ac.26:18]

15

Miracles to Shake the World

W*HEN THEY HAD PRAYED, the place was shaken where they were assembled together...and with great power* [of the Holy Ghost] *the apostles gave witness of the resurrection of the Lord Jesus: and great grace was upon them all.*[Ac.4:31,33]

These were preachers with power—they were *witnesses with evidence.*

And by the hands of the apostles were many signs and wonders wrought among the people ...believers were the more added to the Lord, **multitudes** *both of men and women.*[Ac.5:12,14] —*about three thousand souls...*[Ac.2:41] and *about five thousand...*[Ac.4:4]

Why were these multitudes added to the Lord? Because of the signs and wonders that were done in His Name.

The Early Church succeeded because of their commitment *to obey God rather than men.*[Ac.5:29] They said, We *cannot but speak the things which we have* **seen** *and* **heard.**[Ac.4:20]

They had **seen** Jesus heal the sick, cast out devils, give sight to the blind, raise up paralytics and bless the poor. They were His *witnesses.*

They had **heard** Him say: *The things which I do, you shall do also.*[Jn.14:12] *Go preach the gospel, heal the sick and cast out devils.*[Mk.16:15-18] *As My Father has sent me into the world, even so send I you.*[Jn.20:21]

They had *seen* His example and had *heard* His orders to emulate Him. Therefore, they said, *we cannot but speak the things which we have* **seen** *and* **heard**.[Ac.4:20]

Thank God that, as gospel messengers today, we can give that same witness to the people of this 21st century.

Jesus sent us to *take this gospel to all nations as a witness with evidence.*[Mat.24:14] Only men and women full of faith and the power of the Holy Ghost can do this.

Nothing can substitute for *this gospel with evidence.* There is no alternative for the *demonstration of the Holy Spirit and of power.*[1Cor.2:4]

It is the *witness with evidence* that convinces. One manifestation of God's miraculous power is worth a thousand lectures. One miracle is worth a thousand sermons.

A spiritual awakening swept Jerusalem when Peter and John lifted the notable cripple to his feet, and he was miraculously healed.

A similar spiritual awakening swept Puerto Rico during the first mass miracle crusade that we conducted—in 1950. Juan Santos was a notable cripple who had been shot through the spine. For sixteen years he had walked with his hands, swinging his paralyzed body between his arms. During the crusade, Jesus lifted him to his feet and he was perfectly restored. When the city became aware of the news, thousands of people believed the gospel.

During one of our crusades, a blind, demented and paralyzed beggar, known by almost everyone in the city, was instantly healed. The people of that area *gave heed to what we preached.*[Ac.8:6] That beggar was *proof* that our teaching was biblical. His case was *evidence* that the gospel we proclaimed was true.

During one of our crusades in eastern Africa, the whole province was spiritually aroused and many thousands of people turned to the Lord when a little boy, Simeon, who was born without eyeballs, received a creative miracle. New eyeballs were formed within a few hours and his sight became normal.

The provincial commissioner told us that the news of that creative miracle had spread across the province, and that it had convinced thousands of people, including village chiefs, and even some witchdoctors, to believe on Jesus Christ.

This gospel of the Kingdom was preached as a *witness – with evidence.*

When the Earth Shook

During our crusade in Lubumbashi, Katanga, Congo, such power from God came upon the multitudes as they listened to the gospel, that **the earth literally shook**, as it did when the Early Church believers were *filled with the Holy Ghost, and spoke the word of God with boldness.* The Bible says, ***the place was shaken where they were assembled together.***[Ac. 4:30-31]

The earth shook so fiercely in that Lubumbashi crusade that thousands of people ran in all directions. That area had never experienced any kind of an earthquake, and it was felt nowhere else in the city. It required several minutes to calm the mass of people and to reassemble them.

God gave *witness* to the truth of the Gospel being proclaimed, just as He did in the epoch of the Early Church.

Biblical Miracles Today

This book was first written in the late

1970s. Now I have updated information and have edited some of the text in order to improve the grammar and the writing style.

Not long ago, I returned from ministry in ten major cities of Russia; in cities of Ukraine, Kazakhstan, Poland, Estonia, Bulgaria, Kyrgyzstan; Thailand, Republic of Congo and Ivory Coast. We have witnessed the same miracles in each gospel crusade that have been manifested during six decades of our global evangelism ministry.

In one of our crusades, a crippled beggar who had dragged his body on the ground for thirty years, was miraculously restored. Thousands of people believed on Christ when they saw how this notable cripple was made whole.

Jesus and His gospel have never changed. When His message is proclaimed in this century, *in demonstration of the Spirit and of power* [1Cor.2:4] as the Apostle Paul did, it is confirmed by the miraculous.

When Christ's followers *went forth, and preached every where, the Lord worked with them, confirming the word with signs following,*[Mk.16:20] and He does the same in this century.

Believers in the Early Church were successful. Whole cities were affected. Multitudes believed on Christ. *So mightily grew the word of God and prevailed.* [Ac.19:20]

Since *Jesus Christ is the same yesterday, today, and forever,*[Heb.13:8] when anyone proclaims His Word with simple faith and, acts on His promises, he or she will realize the same results in this century.

Our Lord always confirms *this gospel of the Kingdom* with miraculous evidence. *Believers were added to the Lord, multitudes of both men and women.*[Ac.5:14]

16

Miracles Around the World

WE KNOW WHAT IT MEANS to proclaim the gospel in childlike simplicity to multitudes in more than a hundred nations during over six glorious decades.

I know what it means *to obey God rather than men.*[Ac.5:29] I have done it.

I know what it means to be demeaned and condemned because one dares to act on God's word of promise. Critics have done that to me.

But I also know that faith wins and that biblical courage defeats every enemy.

I have felt the pulse beat of suffering humanity throughout our despairing world. And by the grace and power of God, I have been instrumental in persuading hundreds of thousands of wonderful people to believe on Jesus Christ.

I have proven that there is only one way to evangelize our world before Jesus returns. It is to proclaim *this gospel of the Kingdom with evidence* – in the power of the Holy Spirit, so that it is confirmed by miracles.

I am convinced that people, regardless of race or color, want to know about the God of miracles. The Bible says, *He has made of one blood all nations of people to dwell on all the face of the earth.*[Ac.17:26] They all have the same hunger for God who confirms His Word and fulfills His promises with signs, miracles, and wonders.

I have proclaimed Christ's gospel to Hindus, Muslims, Shintoists, Confucians, animists, fetichists, and to peoples of innumerable tribal religions.

I have shared this gospel in the cold North and in the deep South, in the traditional East and in the industrialized West.

I have taught the Good News of Christ

to the educated and to the illiterate, to people of all colors — black, red, yellow, brown, and white.

One thing I know: *All* people of *all* races, of *all* nations and of *all* creeds, have the same hunger for truth. They are ready to accept the Christ of the gospels and to serve Him when they see His Word confirmed by signs and miracles.

While pious theologians warn people to *"beware of false prophets and deceivers,"* multiplied thousands of souls are turning from traditional, empty religions to serve the Living God when they hear the gospel preached with *evidence.*

Whoever warns against false miracles should at least produce the genuine ones. Moses did, Elijah did, Peter did and Paul did.

17

Miracles for Everybody

*THERE IS NO DIFFERENCE between the Jew and the Greek: for the same Lord over all is rich unto **all that call upon him**.*

*For **whosoever** shall call upon the name of the Lord shall be saved.* Rom.10:12-13

Miracles are for everybody. The gospel is for everyone, for the entire world, for every creature, for every nation, for **whosoever**. *Everything that Christ died to provide is available to everyone for whom He died. There are no exceptions with God.*

If ten thousand non-Christians hear the gospel of salvation, believe it, repent of their sins and accept Jesus Christ as their personal savior by faith, **every one** of them will receive the gift of salvation.

If ten thousand sick people hear Christ's healing gospel, believe it, resist their sickness and accept Jesus Christ as their personal Healer by faith, *everyone* of them will be healed—either instantly or from the time that they believe God's promises, their sicknesses will die at the roots, and they will begin to recover.

Jesus died for every human person. He paid the price for everyone to be able to come to God and to receive His gift of *Life*. That is the *Good News* that we proclaim to *all the world*.Mk.16:15

18

Miracles for You

JESUS SAID, *Preach the gospel to EVERY creature.*[Mk.16:15] That includes you.

What is the "gospel?" It is the Good News of what Jesus accomplished for every person in His substitutionary death on the Cross.

He bore *your* sins so you do not need to bear them—so that you can be forgiven **now**.[1Pet.2:24] He did that for *every person* who has sinned against God—including **you**.

He bore *your* diseases so you do not need to bear them—so that you can be healed **now**.[Mat.8:16-17; Isa.53:4-5] He did that for *every sick person*—including **you**.

Everything Jesus Christ did in His death as our *Substitute*, He did so that we can never be required to do it.

That is why miracles are for you.

Jesus paid for our sins, assumed our guilt and endured our penalty in His death, so that you and I can have His *Life*.

Jesus bore our diseases and carried our sicknesses, in our place, so that you and I can have the health of His *Life*.

Jesus assumed our sinful nature — was made to become sin for us, so that you and I can receive His righteousness.[2Cor. 5:21]

Therefore, every miracle He died to provide is for you and for me **now**.

He took our sins and **now** He gives us His righteousness.[2Cor.5:21]

He bore our diseases and **now** He gives us His health.[Isa.53:4,5]

He carried away our weaknesses and gives us His strength **now**.

He has already taken our sins. Believe it and embrace His salvation, by faith, right **now**.

He has already taken our diseases. Believe it and accept the fact that He bore them in your place, so that **you** can be healed **now**.

Everything that Christ accomplished in His vicarious death on the Cross is part of the "gospel" — part of the "Good News." *It is for "every creature" right* **NOW** *— and that includes* **YOU**.

This is the gospel that we preach *with evidence.* This is the gospel that Jesus Christ confirms with signs and wonders. This is the gospel that is *the power of God unto salvation to EVERY ONE that believes it.*Rom.1:16

If *you* are not included, then no one can be included. If salvation is not for *you*, then it can be for no one. If healing is not provided for *you*, then it is not provided for anyone.

All of God's provisions are for **you!**

If you have not accepted Christ by faith or if you need His miracle blessings, *NOW* is the accepted time... *NOW* is the day of salvation[2Cor.6:2] for **YOU**.

Now is the time that God accepts to fulfill His promise and to receive anyone who believes into His Royal Family. **Now** is the time for **YOU** to accept all of the provisions and blessings that Jesus died to provide for **YOU**.

The Bible says, *AS MANY as received Him, to them gave He power to become the children of God.*[Jn.1:12] That includes **YOU**—right **NOW**.

The Bible says, *AS MANY as touched him were made whole.*[Mk.6:56] That includes **YOU**—right **NOW**.

The *MISSION* Of Christianity

THE GLOBAL MISSION of Christianity is to witness of Christ and of His resurrection to *the entire world* – to *every creature.*^{Mk.16:15} The Apostle Paul said, *Whoever shall call on the name of the Lord shall be saved.*^{Rom.10:13}

T.L. and Daisy Osborn shared a worldwide ministry together for over five decades, before her demise in 1995. T.L. resolved to continue his global ministry to multitudes.

The Osborn daughter, Dr. LaDonna, assumed a prominent role in the leadership of the Osborn world ministry. As the fame of her preaching ministry has spread, she has become involved in her own transevangelical seminars and mass miracle crusades in new fields of the world such as *Russia*, nations of *French-speaking Africa, Eurasia* and the world's largest nation, *China.*

As CEO of *OSBORN Ministries Int'l.*, LaDonna's expertise is making possible the expansion of this ministry in nations around the world. Learn more about the Osborn Global Outreaches through their website, *www.osborn.org.*

The Osborns have reached millions for Christ in over a hundred nations during more than six decades. This ministry-brief is included here to inspire young believers that they, too, can carry the *gospel torch into all the world.*Mk.16:15

Mass Miracle Evangelism

Tommy Lee Osborn and Daisy Marie Washburn were married in Los Banos, California in 1942, at the ages of 17 and 18. In 1945 they went to India as missionaries but were unable to convince the people of these ancient religions—Muslims and Hindus—about Christ. They had not yet discovered the truths about miracles. They returned to the USA dismayed and disheartened—but not dissuaded.

Soon after their demoralizing return home, the Lord appeared to them both, at different times, as they searched for the answer to their dilemma. Then they began to discover the Bible truths that create faith for biblical miracles. They had learned in India that for people of non-Christian nations to believe the gospel, they must witness miracle proof that Jesus Christ is alive today.

They discovered that signs, miracles and wonders are essential to convincing *non*-Christian nations about the gospel. *Jesus was…**approved of God** among people by **miracles** and **wonders** and **signs**, which God did by Him in the midst of the people.* Ac.2:22

These dynamic truths created in their spirits fresh faith in God's Word. With this new lease on life and having discovered the scriptural facts about miracles, they *re*-launched their soulwinning saga in 1949—this time in the Caribbean island-nation of Jamaica.

During thirteen weeks of ministry there, hundreds of biblical miracles confirmed their preaching. Over a hundred deaf-mutes were healed; over ninety totally blind people received sight; hundreds of crippled, paralyzed and lame people were restored; and most important of all, nearly ten thousand souls received Jesus Christ as their Savior.

That success motivated their new global ministry, proclaiming the gospel to multitudes. In the era when so-called "*Third World*" nations were mostly *colonized* by European governments, the Osborns pioneered the concept of *Mass Miracle Evangelism.* Such methods had not been witnessed since the epoch of the Early Church. T.L. and Daisy addressed audiences of tens of thousands throughout the dangerous years of *nationalism* when foreign political domination was being repulsed by the awakening "*Third World*" nations.

Their example inspired national men and women, globally, to arise from their restrictive past, and to become leading gospel messengers and church builders in the unevangelized nations of the world. Many of them are numbered among the most distinguished and successful Christian leaders today.

The largest churches in the world are no longer in America or Europe. They are being raised up by anointed and talented national pastors. Single churches in Africa seat 50,000 plus people under one roof. To God be the glory.

Global Evangelism Concepts

During T.L. and Daisy's unprecedented years as an evangelism team, they inaugurated numerous programs to reach the *un*-reached. Their concept of *National Missionary Assistance* resulted in them sponsoring over 30,000 national preachers as full time missionaries to unevangelized tribes and villages where new, self-supporting churches became established globally.

The Osborn literature is published in 132 languages. Their DocuMiracle crusade films, audio and video cassettes, and their digital productions (including Bible courses), are produced in over 70 languages and are circulated around the world.

They have provided airlifts and huge shipments of literature and of soulwinning tools for gospel ministries abroad. They have furnished scores of four-wheel drive vehicles equipped with films, projectors, screens, generators, public-address systems, audio cassettes and cassette players, plus literature for reaching the un-reached.

Publishing The Gospel

Dr. Daisy's five major books are *pacesetters* in Christian literature for women— *unique examples of **inclusive** language that consistently addresses both genders.*

T.L. has authored over 20 major books. He wrote his first, HEALING THE SICK, during their mission to Jamaica in 1950. Now in its 46th edition, it is a global favorite, used as a Bible School text book in many nations.

The publisher calls HEALING THE SICK *A Living Classic*—a faith-building bestseller since 1950. Over a million copies are in print, circulating healing truth throughout the world.

Their Global Saga

In T.L.'s eighth decade of life, the Osborn ministry continues to expand. Following Daisy's demise, T.L. has continued his global evangelism crusades, and his daughter, Dr. La Donna, has expanded her ministries of evangelism and of church leadership to nearly every continent as she carries the *torch of the gospel* into this century's new frontiers.

Like the Apostle Paul, LaDonna says, *I am not ashamed of the gospel of Christ, for it is the power of God to salvation to everyone who believes.*[Rom.1:16]

She believes that *the World is the **Heart** of the Church,* and *the Church is the **Hope** of the World.* She contends that without the *World,* the *Church is **meaningless*** and without the *Church,* the *World is **hopeless.***

Colonialism
Nationalism
Globalism/Evangelism

Dr. LaDonna Osborn knows the ministry of World Evangelism. Since childhood, she has lived on the front lines of global soulwinning—from the days of *colonialism,* through the turbulent years of *nationalism,* and into this century of *globalism, mass evangelism* and *national Church growth.*

The Osborns hold forth these simple truths:

1) That the Bible is as valid today as it ever was;

2) That the divine calling for every believer is to witness of Christ to the *un*converted;

3) That every soul won to Christ can become His representative; and

4) That miracles, signs and wonders are what distinguish Christianity from being just another philosophical religion.

To demonstrate these biblical issues is the essence of the global *MISSION of Christianity.*

Speaking for Dr. LaDonna and for himself, T.L. quotes Paul: *The ministry we have received of the Lord is to testify to the gospel of the grace of God;* Ac.20:24 *to preach the gospel in the regions beyond.* 2Cor.10:16

The Osborns' testimony is recorded for posterity in their 512 page unique pictorial, *THE GOSPEL ACCORDING TO T.L. AND DAISY.*

The history of the Osborn ministry is also recorded in their unique and historical 24-volume *Encyclo-Biographical Anthology.* It contains more than 23,000 pages, 30,946 photos, 636 *Faith Digest* magazines, 2,024 pages of personal, hand-written diary notes, 1,011 pages of Osborns' news letters, 1,062 pages of unpublished historical data about their world ministry, 2,516 world mission reports, and 6,113 Christian ministry reports.

These 24 giant tomes span over six feet of shelf space and have taken their place in the archives and libraries of institutions of higher learning around the world, including such renowned Universities as Cambridge, Oxford, ORU, Regent, Fuller (plus many more), and the archives of many leading denominational headquarters.

❋ ❋ ❋

• The Osborns' continuing passion: *To express and propagate the gospel of Jesus Christ to all people throughout the world.*

• Their tenet for action: *No one deserves to hear the gospel repeatedly before everyone has heard it at least once.*

• Their motto: *One Way—Jesus;*
One Job—Evangelism.

• Their guiding principle: *Every Christian believer—a witness for Christ.*

The witness is expressed best by the words of the Apostle John: *We bear record of the Word of God, and of the testimony of Jesus Christ, and of the things that we have seen.*[Rev.1:2] *We...testify of these things and have written them: and we know that our testimony is true.* [Jn.21:24]

GLOBAL PUBLISHER

OSBORN PUBLICATIONS
P.O. Box 10
Tulsa, OK 74102 USA

❖❖❖

FRENCH DISTRIBUTOR

POSITIVE CONNEXION
BP 2072
51073 Reims Cedex, France

❖❖❖

GERMAN PUBLISHER

SHALOM — VERLAG
Pachlinger Strrasse 10
D-93486 Runding, CHAM, Germany

❖❖❖

PORTUGUESE PUBLISHER

GRACA EDITORIAL
Caixa Postal 1815
Rio de Janiero–RJ–20001, Brazil

❖❖❖

SPANISH PUBLISHER

LIBROS DESAFIO, Apdo. 29724
Bogota, Colombia

(For Quantity Orders, Request Discount Prices.)